Stereotypes and Labels

The Price We Pay for Tags

Kirby A. Manager, Ph.D.

Stereotypes and Labels

KAM Media Services

P.O. Box 90321

Raleigh NC, 27675

ISBN 978-0-9839304-1-9

Printed and bound in the United States of America

Stereotypes and Labels

Also by Kirby A. Manager

★ *Media Caricature of African Coolness: How to Talk About Africa and Look Cool*

To all who sweat for a just world

Table of Contents

Labels That Kill 11

It's just HIV! 11

Missed Opportunities 22

Misfired Zeal 27

Hard Choices 28

The Repercussions not Considered 29

What Would Jesus Do? 35

This Aid is Foreign 43

Not This Fellowship 43

LABELS THAT KILL

It's just HIV!

There was a time in my life when, if you told me somebody was HIV positive, drugs or prostitution would come to my mind immediately. I lived with this mindset for quite a number of years. I didn't see it as a problem because I knew many people who shared these thoughts. I recall a friend who contracted HIV. In the latter stages of his life, he was completely abandoned by his family, perhaps for being sinful and, thus, merely paying for his sins.

A few years back, I came to realize I also lived with a virus. Mine was not the virus that dwells in the blood, but its variant that inhabits the mind. Its effects were devastating: a troubled, preju- diced mindset about HIV and other sexually- transmitted diseases. Like its variant which I feared, this wasn't an easy-to-treat illness. So I lived with the destructive and erosive ulcer of my thoughts for years.

I first heard about HIV in 1986. I was a young boy in Ghana at that time. Most Sundays, at church, I attended the children's Sunday school service. But, on this Sunday, there was an announcement that representatives from the Ministry of Health would be visiting, so we were going to have a joint service. It was common, in those days, for the government and other public officials to employ the church to disseminate information to the public. It was the cheapest and most effective way to get the message across. You needed only to call upon the local caretaker of the church to reserve some time on the Sunday worship schedule.

Our guests for this Sunday were a team of nurses and public health professionals, sent by the government to tour communities and educate them about the new discovery, HIV. This was not a bad idea, after all. At that time, information available on HIV was scant and full of half-truths.

We've learned quite a lot about HIV in the past quarter century. Even though it was generally effective for the government and local authorities to use the church to educate the communities on issues, it came at a price. The healthcare professionals, in this case, came to sow the seeds. It was left to the laymen of the church to water and nurture the information to see it grow. Depending on what the issue was, the local church could be very valuable in playing this role. Other cases could be too delicate to leave in the hands of unsupervised laymen.

I was young then. Looking back, I'm embarrassed by how much misinformation we were fed both then and in the years that followed. I'm not necessarily describing the situation in my local church but within the church as an institution.

Week after week, HIV was presented to us as a disease that afflicts sinners—those individuals who disobeyed the Word of God. It was nothing less than God's retribution for deviant lifestyles and a warning to return to God. Like most people, I imbibed this into my spirit. For years, I saw people living with HIV as simply paying for their transgressions. The most effective way to warn someone to stay away from sex was to threaten HIV as a penalty. Maybe that wasn't all bad but it still tarred HIV sufferers with the stigma of having sinned and, thus, forced to pay for those transgressions.

Then I began to "grow". I went to college, then graduate school, where I had the opportunity to meet and know run-of-the-mill people like me living more decent lives than I did but who were unfortunate enough to have HIV. Then, things begin to change in me. The faulty mindset I had been living with for years got to me. As a result of my experiences, I discarded the childish thoughts (I Corinthians 13.11). It's not that easy to be healed of a disease that affects a thought process. However, I'm glad education and experience won the battle. You cannot arrive at the truth until you reject formulae and stereotypes.

Many have contracted the virus through the 'sinful' ways we know of, and many more live with the virus for other reasons. Some of those reasons are things we all do everyday and take for granted. One of these people is a girl named Elizabeth Matambanadzo. Elizabeth is from Zimbabwe. Her story appeared in the UN *IRIN News* on January 24, 2010.

Speaking to IRIN, Elizabeth said,

My mother passed away when I was five and my father when I was ten. I have been staying with my grandmother since then. I tested HIV positive in 2008 when I was sixteen after being sick for a long time. I developed sores all over my body that wouldn't heal even after taking medicine. My grandmother and I were always in and out of hospital. I missed a lot of school. At first doctors thought I had diabetes since the sores were not healing.

After the diabetes test came back negative, the doctor recommended an HIV test. At first my grandmother was against the idea, but after some time she agreed. I was shocked when the result came back positive because I had never had sex. My grandmother cried too, she was very sad, but the doctor explained that I may have been born HIV positive. I was very angry and blamed my parents for giving me this disease. I was immediately put on antiretroviral drugs [ARVs] and my sores healed… I feel very strong and healthy… all I want is to continue helping other people affected and infected by HIV/AIDS in my community.

This story of a real human being's HIV makes

a difference. It completely changed the way I

view folks with HIV. They aren't different from

neighbors with diabetes and hypertension. They

are friends, teachers, nurses, athletes, and even

pastors. My hope is that this book may, perhaps,

change the way you see that friend, family member, or neighbor with HIV just as it surely changed the way I see them and interact with them.

UN Secretary-General Ban Ki Moon once said,

> Stigma remains the single most important barrier to public action. It is the main reason why too many people are afraid to see a doctor to determine whether they have the disease, or to seek treatment if so. It helps make AIDS the silent killer, because people fear the social disgrace of speaking about it or taking easily available precautions. Stigma is a chief reason why the AIDS epidemic continues to devastate societies around the world.

Globally, it is estimated that 7,400 people are infected every day with HIV. A significant proportion of these live in sub-Saharan Africa.

Stigmatization of HIV rooted in cultural and religious attitudes may be sending as many people to their graves as the condition itself. HIV is normally associated with behaviors that are shunned by society. These include: prostitution, drugs, homosexuality, and infidelity. In fact, in some communities, HIV, prostitution, and promiscuity are synonyms. I was in a discussion with a college friend when we began to talk about HIV and societal attitudes related to it. He asked a question later in the conversation when I said over 5000 people are infected with HIV everyday. He asked me whether I don't think that some of these figures are just thrown out to deter people from engaging in a homosexual lifestyle. Underlying my friend's question is the gay-HIV connec-

tion.

Unfortunately, stigmatization hurts all of us: the patient, the family, and the community as a whole. Early detection is vital to managing the HIV condition. However, fear of stigmatization makes it difficult for people to go for check ups and testing even when these services are accessible, and often free. It is as difficult to fight the stigma and stereotypes associated with HIV as it is to fight the virus. If we all join the fight, one person at a time, we shall one day overcome both the stigma and the disease.

After all, it's just HIV!

Missed Opportunities

I can't end this chapter without telling this story which a good friend shared with me. It concerns his sister. We were discussing the case of a woman who was beaten to death in Ghana late in 2010 on suspicion of being a witch and the role some churches play in perpetrating this scourge. It was then that my friend digressed to talk about his sister, to whom I'll refer as Joy.

Joy is positive, full of energy and zeal for her Lord. She's her pastor's favorite and had hoped that, "The Goodness of the Lord shall follow her all the days of her life."

But pain in Joy's breast couldn't be regressed with aspirin and regular pain medications. As the pain and concern mounted, she went to see the doctor. You know how the story ended. Through advice from Joy's doctor, she had a mastectomy to remove her breast to prevent the cancer from spreading to other organs.

It's been nearly two decades since Joy had her breast removed but startlingly, but until recently, the only people who knew of her situation were herself, her husband, and her children. Joy is not merely a private person. She has worked so hard to keep her procedure a secret because, like most people in the small communities, she has been preached to over and over again, that cancer is a spiritual illness, a demonic oppression. And for someone who is regarded as a 'sister-on-fire' for

Lord, the last thing she wants is to let folks, especially her church members, know is that she's had cancer, that her Lord couldn't deliver her from the evil spirits. Divulging that information would occur, literally, over her dead body.

In some parts of the word, Joy is just one of the few women who get the rare chance to have such early diagnosis and the grace to live for another twenty years. The majority of cases are never diagnosed. Those that are diagnosed may go untreated because families are unable to afford the treatment. Early detection is key in this battle. Joy could have used her own experience to save many thousands of women. Unfortunately, because of the stigma attached to the disease, rooted in cultural beliefs and compounded by religious labels, she hasn't been of help to a single woman. This is a disaster. And it's not funny.

MISFIRED ZEAL

Politics mixed with religion is always explosive and can be very destructive. In fact, in most cases, it is.

The transmutation of evangelical zeal into some suburb of Christian practice in the West has consequences both at home and abroad. Overseas, it's scary because, in otherwise stable and understanding societies, it's supplanting venerable time-honored systems.

Hard Choices

Recently, there have been waves of incidents where gullible politicians from some African countries, under pressure from religious organizations in the United States, have pushed to enact legislation that could have dire consequences for individuals and upon the stability of societies. One of these is the pressure to pass legislation to execute "suspected" homosexuals in Uganda.

In November 2010, Ugandan M.P., David Bahati, member of the National Resistance Movement, with financial and other support from a politically-connected Christian organization in the United States, sponsored a bill that will impose the death penalty on suspected gay people. The death penalty. Not jail time.

Again, the Prime Minister of Kenya, Mr. Raila Odinga, on Nov 29, 2010, declared a national crackdown on homosexuals. He called upon the police to arrest and jail anyone 'suspected' of being a homosexual. In a region where a child dies of malaria every thirty to forty-five seconds, isn't this a shameful misplacement of priorities?

The Repercussions not Considered

Policies such as those proposed by the Kenyan Prime Minister and the Ugandan M.P. with foreign aid have repercussions beyond what these short-sighted politicians foresee at the time when they're under the zeal. Consider the legislation to execute suspected homosexuals in Uganda and the directive for the police to arrest such individuals in Kenya. Since HIV is automatically associated with homosexuality in some of these cultures, individuals living with HIV are likely to suffer an additional screening for homosexual inclination and, hence, the consequences.

These regrettable measures are certain to encourage bullying in local schools and work places and to create a hostile environment rather than an atmosphere of belonging and safety. When children are suspected of being different, by whatever criteria, they are often subjected to different treatments which could include physical and verbal harassment by the friends. This could lead to their staying out of school. Children who are treated differently by their peers often suffer from low self-esteem. Some carry the effects of mistreatment into adulthood.

It is particularly disturbing when 'foreign aid' is offered to help shape cultures and societies.

Different societies in Africa have different mechanisms to handle practices that they deem foreign or unacceptable. Homosexuality is among those practices. These systems, though not flaw-less, have worked for some communities over centuries. An Idi-Amin-style crackdown, such as is proposed in Uganda, is unnecessary and ill-advised.

Stereotypes and Labels

African communities don't need foreign aid to ward off an unwelcome lifestyle. Unfortunately, like it or hate it, foreign aid to fight homosexuality in Africa is easier to secure than assistance to drill wells for potable water for rural communities.

An anti-homosexual seminar held in Kampala, Uganda in March 2009 featured an American anti-gay evangelist, Scott Lively, and a former gay convert, Caleb Lee Brundidge. Lively is the leader of the Abiding Truth Ministries, an organization classified as a hate group by the Southern Poverty Law Center. Public records haven't provided me with the number of anti-malaria mosquito nets Pastor Scott Lively and Caleb Lee carried with them on their anti-homosexuality mission. An evangelical is supposed to preach love. When is there time to preach love when all the time and efforts are spent on delivering judgment?

Recent events across parts of Africa show that the views of some religious leaders are regarded not merely as models but as images of God by many Christians. Yet these same "images of God" openly express intolerance in several forms without tact. If these views are allowed to permeate these fragile and yet fertile institutions, the effects will be ruinous. Consider Rev. Franklin Graham who is highly respected in many communities and adored as a role model. Yet, he does not hesitate to make highly inflammatory statements regarding Muslims on television. Imagine young men and women 'on-fire' for the Lord employing this as their benchmark! Religious violence claims the lives of hundreds around the world. This occurs in Nigeria, Egypt, Sudan and many other places. Respected and adored figures in the faith have an obligation to communicate the message that we can live together in harmony regardless of racial or religious differences. Even if they don't really mean it and it's just for the television, their words have the power to save many lives.

I'm not writing as an activist for any particular faction. What I'm worried about is the instability these groups may cause in those societies. Also, it's not the desire to fight off what the politicians and community leaders see as the un-healthy intrusion of western lifestyles that bothers me. What I'm worried about—and I hope you, too—is that a group from a powerful country like the U.S. is allowed to use financial power and political connections to dictate legislation in other countries by bribing gullible politicians. This cannot be labeled evangelicalism. Or it's not evangelism as taught by the greatest evangelist, Saint Paul.

What Would Jesus Do?

The aforementioned highlights the subtle intrusion of the fringes of religion into politics. Some will call it fundamentalism, often cloaked in the garments of evangelicalism. Throughout the past few years, we've witnessed media personnel and politicians with hazardous and extreme views on important issues collectively classified as "evangelicals". It appears it's when a person is adamantly intolerant and defines everything based only on his/her views and provides a simplistic answer to the most complicated question of society that he/she qualifies to be an evangelical. This wasn't always the case and it doesn't have to be so.

Year after year, it seems as though we create a space in the political arena to be occupied by the candidate who fits this description of an evangelical or something close to it. And because the competition to occupy that space is fierce, the most outrageous always wins. But do they win for Christ?

One of my college colleagues used this quote as his moral yardstick. He had it written on a 4" by 6" postcard and posted on his student bunk bed: *I have become all things to all people so that by all possible means I might save some.*

This friend, like the majority of the "on-fire brothers and sisters" I knew then, understood that it was easier to win souls when the soul winner appears to identify with the lost and comes down to where they are.

On the morning of Saturday, March 26, 2010, over a cup of coffee, I was reading my copy of the February issue of *Drug Discovery News*. On page ten of the magazine, Professor Peter T. Kissinger, CEO of Prosolia and Professor of Chemistry at Purdue University, asked, "How can one be tolerant and evangelical simultaneously?"

At first thought, I found the question to be superfluous and misplaced. I argued that evangelicalism and tolerance have never been irreconcilable, at least in my experience. Again, I wondered why he'd ask this question, particularly in a scientific discussion. The evangelicals I knew were the most tolerant of Christians because of their zeal to bring outsiders into the fold.

While it's a fact that the term *evangelical* is overused in today's dialogue, the number of people who call themselves evangelical simply because they oppose or support one issue in society is also increasing. Actually, a 2008 public opinion poll by Ellison Research showed that fourteen percent of people who call themselves evangelical don't even know what the term means. Half of all Americans don't know what an evangelical is and the others who think they know, cannot agree on its definition.

Evangelicalism now isn't what I thought I knew it to be. To some people, the mention of evangelism connotes some kind of intolerant, judgmental, on-fire religious person. What's worrisome is the speed at which such a model of evangelism is growing and taking over the concept of old-time, common sense evangelicalism. The term is used so indiscriminately, especially on television, that one begins to wonder what it really stands for.

The sad thing is you may as well forget the type of evangelical movement typical of my friend in college. It's gone. The remnants of that movement aren't defending the tradition. The extreme that fit the media stereotype are jumping around and claiming the label. *Evangelical* is derived from the Greek *euangelion*, which means: "gospel" or "good news". This was supposed to represent someone who preaches the good news. That doesn't sound sexy, does it? It's still the definition that you may imagine Saint Paul would make noise about.

Why should you care about this? You should not be worried about who calls himself or herself an evangelical. People have the right to call themselves whatever they want. You should, however, be afraid of the impact on vulnerable societies around the world such as those I mentioned. For instance, in Ghana, where I come from, we have a system where Christians, Muslims, and traditional believers exist in harmony, even though they disagree on a lot of issues. It would only take a handful of fundamentalists, eager to model Pastor Scott Lively's enthusiasm, to tilt the balance.

Malaria kills over two thousand African children every day. One mosquito net, which costs less than ten bucks, could save a family for five years. Perhaps what we need to ask is, "What would Jesus do?"

THIS AID IS FOREIGN

Not This Fellowship

I grew up in a very 'conservative, African' community and in an evangelical family. We attended church every Sunday. There were closed-eye prayers before every meal. Fasting and prayer occurred at least once a month. Next to the Chief, the Priest was the most respected member of our community. "Praise the Lord!" and "Hallelujah!" were the most common greetings and responses on the street. Some of the non-believers, as we used to call them, were more conservative than regular church-goers in New York. Words and phrases such as: *homosexual, lesbian, bisexual,* and *transgender* weren't part of the vocabulary. If you stumbled upon Leviticus 20:13 where it is written, "If a man lies with a man as one lies with a woman, both of them have done what is detestable. They must be put to death; their blood will be on their own heads," either this wouldn't mean much to you, or it might be referring to the Biblical Sodom and Gomorrah.

That was then. Today, in some Sub-Saharan African communities, you dare not read such scriptures in public, thanks to a powerful U.S.

lobbying group that has bribed its way into politics in these countries. Uganda is the poster child.

The group, called The Family, also known as The Fellowship, is one of the most politically connected advocacy groups in the U.S. In some sense, the group has played a positive role in securing American aid to Uganda, spending several million dollars on sex education in the African country. Unfortunately, The Family has, on several occasions, overreached its influence on vulnerable African communities in the countries where they operate. With the money they helped direct into Uganda, they also heavily stressed abstinence from sex as the only means to curb

HIV. This was accompanied by an evangelical reawakening which led to pubic condom burning.

David Bahati , the anti-gay Ugandan M.P., who sponsored the "execute homosexuals bill", has attended The Family's National Prayer Breakfast in the U.S. and is a key figure in the Ugandan Chapter of the Family Prayer Breakfast.

While Mr. Bahati worked hard to get his bill through the Ugandan parliament, a Ugandan newspaper published the list of "top homosexuals" on the front page with a bright yellow banner across it that read: "Hang Them!" They did so to pacify the restless politicians who just couldn't wait. The paper's editor, Giles Muhame, defended the list, stating that he published it to expose

Ugandan gays and lesbians to make it easier for the authorities to arrest them.

It's disturbing that people who have learned to live with all lifestyles in the West are supporting or condoning radical approaches to root out people who chose to live differently in other places.

Why shouldn't Christians in Uganda and other African countries, as well as places like Asia, South America, be able handle such issues within their own traditions? Societies deal with aberrations by their local institutions. Draconian measures such as execution are new. What we have now is an external group preying upon the ignorance and poverty of other communities and the greediness of politicians to reshape the societies in a way that pleases them.

From a religious point of view, does the execution of "sinners" accomplish much? It reminds me of what Jesus said to the men who brought him the sinful woman caught in the act of adultery. "Let him who is without sin cast the first stone."

I'm a chemist. I've initiated scary chemical reactions during my career. Politics plus religion is not one of my favorite reactions. The two don't mix very well. When they do, the product is always an explosive waste.

Acknowledgments

This book is the result of encouragement from many people regarding short articles I wrote on some of the issues discussed in this book. It was the positive comments of these people that inspired me to share my thoughts with the wider public in a book.

I'm also grateful to Catherine Trevelline and the UN IRIN news network for the Elizabeth Matambanadzo story that I was permitted to quote in this book.

Finally, I'm gratefully to my wife and children for their sacrifice while I worked on this book. As it always is, you never how much work it will entail.

About the Author

Kirby A. Manager, PhD. is originally from Ghana but has lived in the United States for the past several years. He earned his Ph. D. in chemistry at the University of Florida, Gainesville. He's a full-time scientist in Pharmaceutical Research & Development. In his spare time, he enjoys reading and writing about issues affecting the developing world and playing soccer with his two boys. He's the author of: *Media Caricature of Africa Coolness: How to Talk About Africa and Look Cool.* He lives in Raleigh, NC